A New Tune A Day
Pop Performance Pieces
for Trumpet

Chord symbols for all pieces are included
for guitar or keyboard accompaniment.

Boston Music Company
part of The Music Sales Group
London/New York/Paris/Sydney/Copenhagen/Berlin/Madrid/Hong Kong/Tokyo

Contents

Published by

Boston Music Company

Exclusive Distributors:

Music Sales Limited

14-15 Berners Street, London W1T 3LJ, UK.

Music Sales Corporation

257 Park Avenue South, New York, NY 10010, USA.

Music Sales Pty Limited

20 Resolution Drive, Caringbah, NSW 2229, Australia.

Order No. BM12694

ISBN: 978-1-78038-512-9

Produced by shedwork.com

Photography by Matthew Ward

Printed in the EU

Your Guarantee of Quality

As publishers, we strive to produce every book to the highest commercial standards. The music has been freshly engraved and the book has been carefully designed to minimise awkward page turns and to make playing from it a real pleasure. Throughout, the printing and binding have been planned to ensure a sturdy, attractive publication which should give years of enjoyment. If your copy fails to meet our high standards, please inform us and we will gladly replace it.

www.musicsales.com

American Pie

Words & Music by Don McLean
© Copyright 1971 Mayday Music, USA.
Universal/MCA Music Limited.
All rights in Germany administered by Universal/MCA Music Publ. GmbH.
All Rights Reserved. International Copyright Secured.

Bad Romance

Words & Music by Stefani Germanotta & RedOne

© Copyright 2009 House Of Gaga Publishing Incorporated/
Songs Of RedOne/Sony/ATV Songs LLC, USA.
Sony/ATV Music Publishing.
All Rights Reserved. International Copyright Secured.

With confidence ♩ = 119
(hi-hat cue)

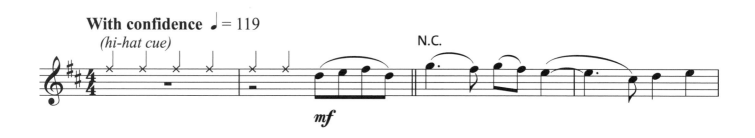

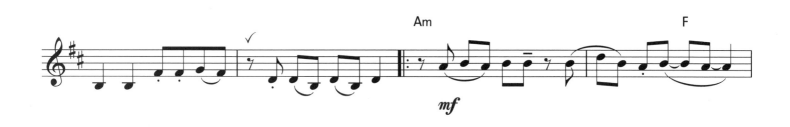

Brown Eyed Girl

Words & Music by Van Morrison
© Copyright 1967 Web IV Music Incorporated, USA.
Universal Music Publishing Limited.
All rights in Germany administered by Universal Music Publ. GmbH.
All Rights Reserved. International Copyright Secured.

Brightly ♩ = 150

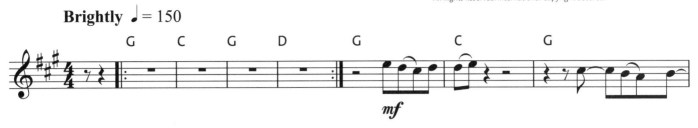

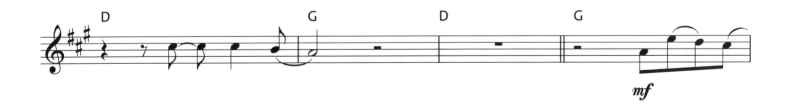

Can't Take My Eyes Off You

Words & Music by
Bob Crewe & Bob Gaudio

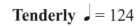

Tenderly ♩ = 124

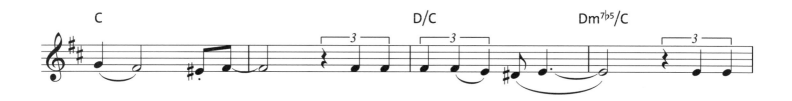

14

Don't Stop Believin'

Words & Music by Steve Perry,
Neal Schon & Jonathan Cain
© Copyright 1981 Weed High Nightmare Music/
Alfred Music Publishing Company Incorporated (75%)/
Lacey Boulevard Music/Sony/ATV Music Publishing (25%).
All Rights Reserved. International Copyright Secured.

Soulfully ♩ = 118

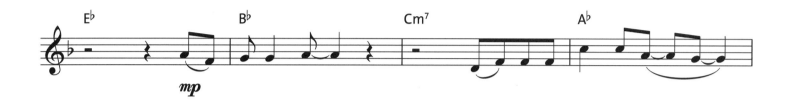

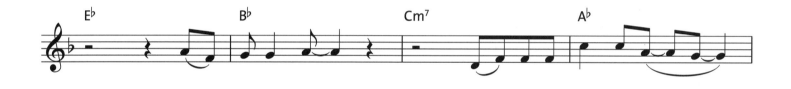

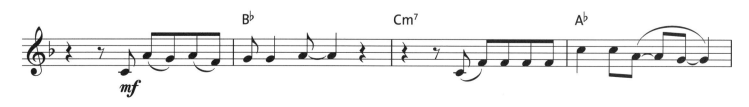

D.S. al Coda

Coda
(guitar solo)

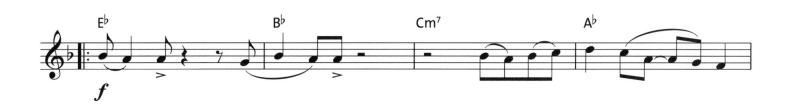

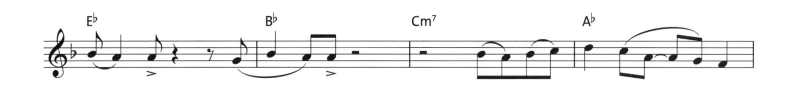

Repeat to fade

Defying Gravity (from the Broadway Musical Wicked)

Words & Music by Stephen Schwartz

Fireflies

Words & Music by Adam Young

© Copyright 2009 Ocean City Park, USA.
Universal/MCA Music Limited.
All Rights Reserved. International Copyright Secured.

Lightly, with a bounce ♩ = 90

N.C.   *1st time optional tin mute, 2nd time open*

mf leggiero

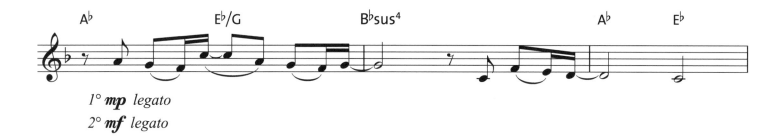

1° *mp* legato
2° *mf* legato

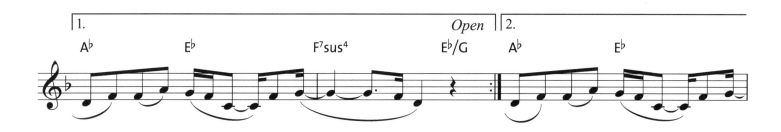

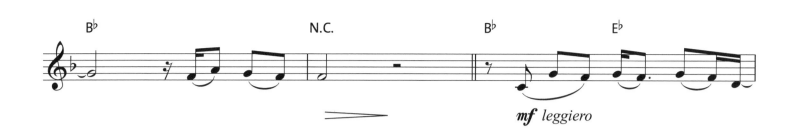

Good Vibrations

Words & Music by Brian Wilson & Mike Love

© Copyright 1966 Sea Of Tunes Publishing Company/Irving Music Incorporated, USA.
Rondor Music International.
All rights in Germany administered by Rondor Musikverlag GmbH.
All Rights Reserved. International Copyright Secured.

I Got You (I Feel Good)

10

I Say A Little Prayer

Words by Hal David
Music by Burt Bacharach

Medium tempo

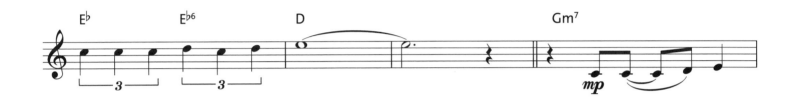

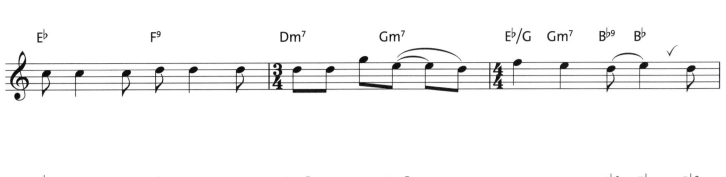

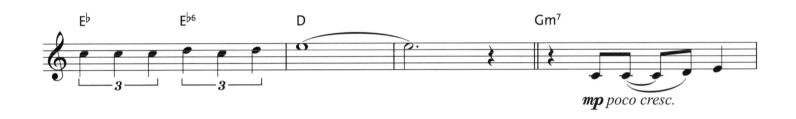

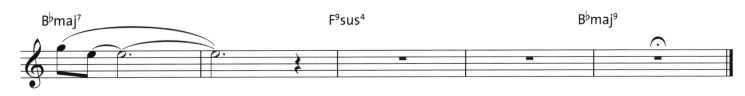

Man In The Mirror

Words & Music by Glen Ballard & Siedah Garrett

(Sittin' On) The Dock Of The Bay

Words & Music by
Otis Redding & Steve Cropper

Son Of A Preacher Man

Words & Music by
John Hurley & Ronnie Wilkins

Take A Bow

Words & Music by Mikkel Eriksen,
Tor Erik Hermansen & Shaffer Smith

D.S. al Coda

Coda

molto rit.

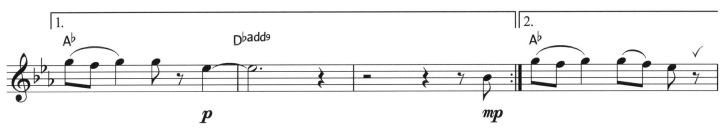

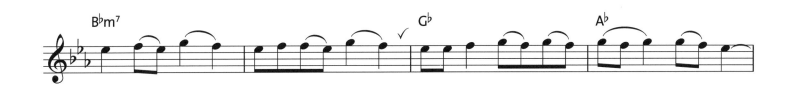

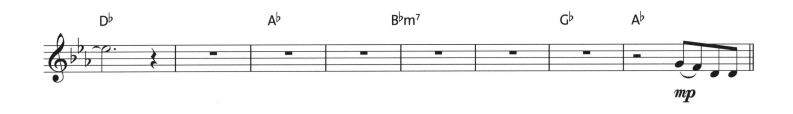

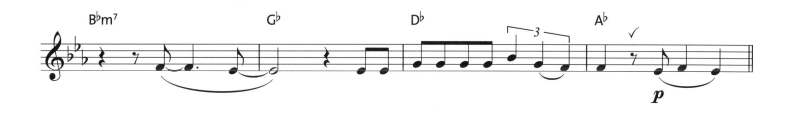

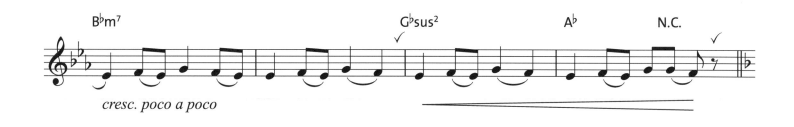

cresc. poco a poco

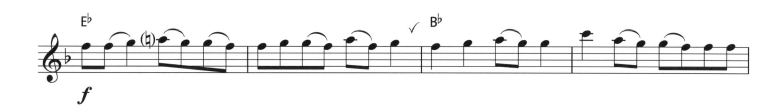

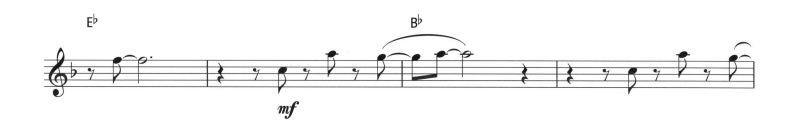

With A Little Help From My Friends

Words & Music by John Lennon & Paul McCartney

CD backing tracks

1. **TUNING NOTE**

2. **AMERICAN PIE**
(McLean)
Universal/MCA Music Limited

3. **BAD ROMANCE**
(Germanotta/RedOne)
Sony/ATV Music Publishing (UK) Limited

4. **BROWN EYED GIRL**
(Morrison)
Universal Music Publishing Limited

5. **CAN'T TAKE MY EYES OFF OF YOU**
(Crewe/Gaudio)
EMI Music Publishing Limited

6. **DON'T STOP BELIEVIN'**
(Perry/Schon/Cain)
Wixen Music UK Ltd/Sony/ATV Music Publishing (UK) Limited

7. **DEFYING GRAVITY**
(Schwartz)
Imagem Music

8. **FIREFLIES**
(Young)
Universal/MCA Music Limited

9. **GOOD VIBRATIONS**
(Wilson/Love)
Universal Music Publishing Limited

10. **I GOT YOU (I FEEL GOOD)**
(Brown)
Lark Music Limited

11. **I SAY A LITTLE PRAYER**
(David/Bacharach)
Universal/MCA Music Limited/Warner/Chappell Music Publishing Limited

12. **MAN IN THE MIRROR**
(Ballard/Garrett)
Universal/MCA Music Limited/Cherry Lane Music Limited

13. **(SITTIN' ON) THE DOCK OF THE BAY**
(Redding/Cropper)
Universal Music Publishing Limited/Warner/Chappell Music Limited.

14. **SON OF A PREACHER MAN**
(Hurley/Wilkins)
Sony/ATV Music Publishing (UK) Limited

15. **TAKE A BOW**
(Eriksen/Hermansen/Smith)
Imagem Music/EMI Music Publishing Limited/
Sony/ATV Music Publishing (UK) Limited

16. **LOVE STORY**
(Swift)
Sony/ATV Music Publishing (UK) Limited

17. **WITH A LITTLE HELP FROM MY FRIENDS**
(Lennon/McCartney)
Sony/ATV Music Publishing (UK) Limited

How to use the CD

The tuning note on track 1 is an A.

After track 1, the backing tracks are listed in the order in which they appear in the book. Look for the 💿 symbol in the book for the relevant backing track.